Thank you

I will opt to not do a survey, but will write this. Have no ill feelings toward teachers learning, I haven't ill feelings toward you.

Everyone has a point of view, it is true!

Everything is not common sense. The best of wishes from Asia still and please enjoy this......

Summer 2012

3 Generations

A grandmother-Minnie Dora Roper
A mother-Frances Roper
A daughter-Asia

1 Mind

A compilation of poetry works

Her thoughts, their thoughts, my thoughts

Asia DSheille

iUniverse, Inc.
Bloomington

3 Generations... A grandmother-Minnie Dora Roper A mother-Frances Roper A daughter-Asia...1 Mind

A compilation of poetry works ...her thoughts, their thoughts, my thoughts

Copyright © 2011 by Asia DSheille.

The views expressed in this work are solely those of the author and do not necessarily reflect the views of the publisher, and the publisher hereby disclaims any responsibility for them.

All rights reserved. No part of this book may be used or reproduced by any means, graphic, electronic, or mechanical, including photocopying, recording, taping or by any information storage retrieval system without the written permission of the publisher except in the case of brief quotations embodied in critical articles and reviews.

iUniverse books may be ordered through booksellers or by contacting:

iUniverse
1663 Liberty Drive
Bloomington, IN 47403
www.iuniverse.com
1-800-Authors (1-800-288-4677)

Because of the dynamic nature of the Internet, any web addresses or links contained in this book may have changed since publication and may no longer be valid. The views expressed in this work are solely those of the author and do not necessarily reflect the views of the publisher, and the publisher hereby disclaims any responsibility for them.

Any people depicted in stock imagery provided by Thinkstock are models, and such images are being used for illustrative purposes only.
Certain stock imagery © Thinkstock.

ISBN: 978-1-4620-4316-3 (sc)
ISBN: 978-1-4620-4317-0 (ebk)

Printed in the United States of America

iUniverse rev. date: 08/17/2011

CONTENTS

FOREWORD vii
FROM MOM: ix
NOW xi
JANUARY 1
FREBRUARY 3
MARCH 5
MARCH 6
APRIL – I THOUGHT OF YOU 8
MAY 10
JUNE 12
SHOUT OUT 14
THE CHILDREN 18
YOUR MARK 19
SHATTERED 20
GOD SPOKE TO ME 21
SUNSHINE 23
UNTITLED (1) 25
TODAY 27
UNTITLED (2) 29
FOR THE GRACE OF GOD
THANK YOU FOR MOTHERS 31

LETTER TO SISTERS: WRITTEN 7/16/04 33
PAST/PRESENT 36
WHAT I WANT TO BE 38
A DEDICATION TO THE
STRUGGLE OF THE BLACK PEOPLE 40
BUDDIES 42
TEACHERS 44
WHY 46
MEN 48
BLACK MAN RUN BUT WHEN DO YOU STOP? 50
GAMES 52
PEOPLE 54
RELIGION 56
GANGS/FEELINGS 58
PEACE 60
IT'S NOT THE FAULT OF A CHILD 62
LOVE AND INSANITY 64
TWO WORLDS 65
A PAIN SO DEEP 67
LIFE AND DEATH 69
GIRL 70
BECAUSE THEY RAPED OUR BABIES 71
SO REMEMBER TO CALL HER BEAUTIFUL 74
WHO IS JESUS? 77

Foreword

Many years ago, Minnie Dora Morrison and Wilbert Hayward Roper created a seed . . . (5 and 4 seeds later), Frances Roper. Frances Roper turned McGill later conceived another seed (2 seeds later), Asia. And this seed, me, well, I'm a seed to be reckoned with . . . .

3 Generations...A grandmother-Minnie Dora Roper A mother-Frances Roper A daughter-Asia...1 Mind

From mom:

. . . My Lord and Savior Jesus Christ, in all his omnipotence allowed certain trials, tests, people, and circumstances to come into my life with just enough words of encouragement which acted like precious water and sunshine to allow this seed to grow into a flower. That flower produced another seed which got planted on firm soil of her own and sprouted into an even bigger flower whose fragrance, I pray, will always fill the air with "Excerpts from Asia."

3 Generations...A grandmother-Minnie Dora Roper A mother-Frances Roper A daughter-Asia...1 Mind

Now

Now I'm not in the mood to write it's been like seven years right? Writing for school and for work, but for what? I'm not lickin' carpet munchin', brown nosin' kissin' butt. Credentials-credentials-What? What am I qualified for not giving a what. Oh I would have typed it and did think it what— Now . . . . then . . . . Now . . . . then—I haven't changed much.

-Asia 2011

January

Bitter, cold wind, marring paints on the house—zero degrees and below feels like what is between you and your spouse.

You are living the hard knock life while your enemies have impunity, and you think in your mind *who is doing this to me?*

The New Year is here and everyone is being hard to deal with, intently they give you problems they want you to be real with.

Your tactic to stray away from provocation leaves you languid and tired from damnation.

You try to ease your mind with some form of exhilaration; maybe if you overdose on pills you'll fulfill your temptation.

Life as you've known it has never seemed like it was in proper succession.

So hell here you come, it seems an easier direction.

Who am I? I am the cold in January, the heat in July.

I lust, sex, steal, judge, kill and lie.

Temptation will fill me.

-Asia 2002

3 Generations...A grandmother-Minnie Dora Roper A mother-Frances Roper A daughter-Asia...1 Mind

F★EBRUARY

This is supposed to be the month of love, hence Valentine's Day.
I try hard and try harder once again not to hate.
You are not here when I need you and I am supposed to love?
You give me the cold shoulder, and kick me out, and expect to receive hugs?
This is supposed to be the time of love and appreciation.
You curse at me, hit me, cheat on me and think this is a good relation?
And brother and mother and my sister too,
We are supposed to be family all year round even February too.
When I need a shoulder to lean on, I look to you,
My family; but then I realize you don't love me too.
There's no love any more someone show me where,
Will I ever find just one person to care?
I showed you love tell me now if I lie.

Asia DSheille

And I can't help but ask when I look for love in return; Why?
Why is it I bend over backwards for others?
When my life is obviously having a drought on lovers.
Has my light not shined bright enough to see
just the little-lest bit of love in February?

-Asia 2002

March

This month of mayhem and undecided minds
A longer winter or nearer spring-you and your thoughts reclined.

Remembering the blistery snowy days
And the long days and long nights away.

Many nights you were all by yourself, alone
Cold and the homeless without shelter or a home.

Reaching for some way an open door.
Crying voices of pain cry out "PAIN NO MORE!"

Hell is what some people felt, they thought it was cold they felt pain in their hearts
And yes there was loss, hunger, loneliness, and sorrow during the month of March

March

You marched in my life unexpectedly-you truly off guarded me. Now march back out.

I asked you once nicely next time I'll shout. You hurt me. You walked, skipped, ran easily right over my feelings.

You toyed with the word love one time too many, now hate for you I have plenty. Alah my God says "forgive thee".

B. S. lies that's all you tell-well goodbye love-I wish you well.

Marching over girl's hearts is what you are accustomed to,
That is not fair! It's not right! What if I played you?

I bet you didn't know your missteps had you marching over that line, yeah it's hard to see when one is love blind. It's thin not hard to cross and it will leave you crying.

Yes darlin' there is a thin line between love and hate-seems cliché' but it's not fake. You my love friend, made it this way. Now I march over you. You I hate. No no—my love has a limit there's no forgiveness today.

-Asia 2002 (revised 2011)

April

I THOUGHT OF YOU

I COULD NOT SLEEP SO I THOUGHT OF YOU AND ALL OF THE TRIFLING THINGS TOO!
I THOUGHT OF YOU WHEN YOU SAID YOU LOVED ME AND I THOUGHT OF YOUR SCORNED INSIDES-SO UGLY.
I THOUGHT OF YOU AND YOUR HEART- THEN REMEMBERED (SILLY ME) YOU DIDN'T HAVE ONE TO START
I THOUGHT OF YOU AND HOW YOU PASSIONATELY KISSED ME AND THE SAME LIPS YOU MADE BLEED WHEN YOU HIT ME
I THOUGHT OF YOU AND HOW WE WERE SUPPOSE TO MAKE A FAMILY-I THOUGHT OF YOUR CHEATING WAYS AND KNEW IT COULD NEVER BE
I THOUGHT OF YOU BECAUSE I COULD NOT SLEEP AND THOUGHT HOW YOUR PHONE

3 Generations...A grandmother-Minnie Dora Roper A mother-Frances Roper A daughter-Asia...1 Mind

CALLS EXCITED ME.
I THOUGHT OF YOU AND STARTED TO CRY-REMEMBERING SLEEPLESS NIGHTS I WANTED TO DIE
I THOUGHT OF YOU IN ALL THOSE OTHER GIRLS ARMS AND PRE-MEDITATED DOING YOU HARM
AND AS I WENT TO THINK ABOUT YOU AGAIN-I HAD TO STOP THINKING TO MYSELF ABOUT YOU ANYHOW BECAUSE THE TEARS WERE POURING.
NO MORE THOUGHTS OF YOU!

-Asia 2002

May

May-day may-day someone help me please. I don't want to submit here am I on my knees
May you please be kind to me? I will love you thick or thin even if you don't love me
May is that month my Auntie was born, family is a funny thing so easily torn
Mayhem what is going on in this world? Boys liking boys-girls liking girls . . .
Mayonnaise children are hungry tuna sandwich seems a simple treat, but only mayonnaise on the bread is what they will eat
    May-day may-day will you allow me to continue why are the children hungry in Haiti and here we have too many menus
    May you please mind someone else's business ask if they are okay,
No we keep so many secrets . . . that's "THE AMERICAN WAY"
    May is that month with Memorial day-remember the places we invaded so with their oil we can play

3 Generations...A grandmother-Minnie Dora Roper A mother-Frances Roper A daughter-Asia...1 Mind

Mayhem what does that word actually mean? Your mother smokes crack, pregnant at sixteen, college for most blacks in 2011 yup still a dream

Mayonnaise whips on the scene, but Kanye doesn't care it seems

May-day May-day, may you help me please?

Asia 2011

June

Well June is the first month in the season of summer, but how did we get seasons four approximately I wonder . . .
That is the case for us living in the United States
So far we do not have a rainy season or monsoon season it seems we never have drought
It seems this is the number one world power so we shouldn't be without—Any who that's not what this poem's about

So yes June is the first month in summer. I've been called a summer baby and made my baby in July hot weather gets me crazy

The beginning of freedom, great weather a possible extension for a Spring-fling
Oh Boy the trouble that summer can bring

Oh optimism, JOY! June can make you sing- the tenth month I bet you didn't think of it as a numerical thing

Babies being made, cards being played, numbers getting saved; souls getting raised, food on grills being placed, backyard bar-b-q days

Yup only the beginning of the summer after the month of May

June is the tune that summer's in the room
Up in a roar crowds at concerts in the grass, screaming more
Not ready to go back to work or school. Vacations have just begun ending up married or mated with June-time fun!

-2011

Shout Out . . .

Can I get to you, T not T ma Bev inspire me, but T-T money crabby cancer you're funny. 3 years after 2 knew you. Kita, Rachael, Zenobia, and Marie too.

What'd they call us BT crew, looking back as a grown-up PEE . . . U

How is Mya Mya Jay Jay my Boo should I shout out their father too? LOL who

Needed something to write on a Sunday nite 2 days til deadline right. Right so shot shots shots shots shots and shout out to all

Bottom to top, Top to Bottom . . .

God, myself, my son can't stop, Mamma daddy wherever you never were

Uncle Louis, Mike, Aunt Nita and Lynda with a Y don't forget her

Cousins cousins don't know them all Sandy Missy Mo Jason my memory is flawed (Ty and Ant)

My babies my babies India Marsha Tay, Shirl Angelique Ashley Aaron in a way Babba Lique

Sam 1 hey Jacob called Israel babe who am I forgetting no one I hope I'll say. Well I think for today I'm done with the writing/typing word play . . . .

I wish I would . . . continue to let myself be taken advantage of by a man one night stand or any bitter woman's plan

I wish I could . . . continue to love the both of you I can't really want to but I shan't act like this isn't effecting me

I wish I would . . . get a break make enough just enough to be on the plate, being a millionaire yup GREAT, but I just want enough for a place to stay

I wish I could . . . stop sinning stay grinning and wrong living soul slippin my mind trippin, while Moscoto sippn half in/out dippin in what's missin'

I wish I would . . . get it together keep it together, do so much more better and not just whatevers clever I too want love forever

I wish I could . . . forgive more, turned un-God's child slut whore, according to definition, fornication pretty brown eyes overatin' still single seats not taken. Wish I could love you, but I'm fakin'

I wish I would . . . forget about why I'm hot, not sin—yes I do

But yet still, tutor and work for free too, toughest children in DC my boos so beat myself up-can't dude want truth it's youth who helps me keep my head up to do what I do

I wish . . . 2011

THE CHILDREN

THE CHILDREN ARE NOT CHILDREN BECAUSE OF THEIR AGE,

THEY ARE BOTH OLD AND YOUNG FILLED UP WITH PAIN.

FATHER, "OH!", THEY ARE CRYING OUT, THEY DO IT IN SILENCE;

THEY CRY THROUGH DRUGS, MURDERS AND MALICIOUS VIOLENCE.

FATHER THE CHILDREN WANT LOVE, I KNOW YOU LOVE THEM AND SHOW THEM ENOUGH.

BUT FATHER YOU ALREADY KNOW,

THEY ARE CHILDREN-THEY NEED TO BE TAUGHT AND THEIR EYES ARE CLOSED.

FATHER I AM TRYING BUT I CAN'T DO IT ALONE,

FATHER THE CHILDREN NEED NOT A HOUSE THEY NEED A HOME.

Your Mark

Hurt over and over again. Nobody's gaining nobody will win.

Is that too negative for you? Well I apologize for not candy coating the truth.

I loved you and depended upon you. I opened up my heart something I said I'd never do.

You never loved me; you just did not want to feel the guilt.

You could have aborted me, I would not have appealed.

But no, you brought me here unwillingly. You hurt me time and again. You put a bruise right through my heart.

You bruised me for life with pain-you've left your mark.

Shattered

I was a glass window. Happy as can be. I got fogged and could not clearly see . . .

You cleaned me.

I was clean again and crystal clear, I could see beautiful things although I could not hear

Yes a glass window, the sun shined on me, the rays on my face was love from he. (G-o-d)

When it rained you placed a shutter here to keep me dry, you didn't let the rain make me teary eyed.

I was a glass window and all of a sudden rocks beat at my heart but it didn't matter . . .

I just knew you were coming to save me. I **was** a window. I got shattered.

God spoke to me

Not only did he breathe breath into me to give me life, but he spoke to me too!

I pulled away, I backslid, I disobeyed, he was angry yet mercifully I was let loose.

He didn't punish me-I punished myself. There's no need in trying to blame God when God really helps.

At the end of my rope, I spoke to others and to myself. I did answer my own questions and some people say that's bad for your health.(talking to yourself)

I wanted to kill myself because my heart did bleed,

But God patched it God's voice were bandages when he spoke to me.

Sunshine

Sunshine, sunshine way up in the sky.

Did anyone ever stop to think why God put you there?

Oh feel the rays; the smell is in the air.

Where do you think the rays come from?

They are from the sun because God placed them there.

Sunshine compare your life with the sun.

Say "Hello there. We are shining today! And there's nothing in this world that's going to make me say, you're gone and not here to stay."

Oh Sun, Oh Sun please, don't go away because you are the main thing in my life today.

Asia DSheille

Even when you are hiding behind the clouds some days, I must keep in mind-*God made it this way.* (Smile)

-Minnie Dora Roper '91

Untitled (1)

Today I got angry, lost control.

I couldn't believe it was happening and I was one frightened soul.

I had allowed myself to get out of control.

Anger came so quickly, I'm sorry to say-No matter how you think, anger will come your way.

LOVE! LOVE! Please don't go away.

I've found a way to mix it so it will last more than a day.

With a dash of kindness and friendship you can cast it away. Add a bit of courage each and every day.

Don't forget to smile it goes a long way.

Asia DSheille

Mix these all together, stir them very well.

I guarantee you one thing. Your love will never stray.

Minnie Dora Roper '91

3 Generations...A grandmother-Minnie Dora Roper A mother-Frances Roper A daughter-Asia...1 Mind

Today

Today I met my mom for the first time in my life

In the past, there was much turmoil, so much strife

But all that is behind me now

And there's one thing I know for sure

My mom's a changed person

She has always loved the Lord

We spent a whole day together,

Secretly I kept hoping time

would somehow stop

But now I know we will be joint Aires in heaven

And will be together forever and ever

Not only did I find my mother,

But I made another discovery

All the attributes that are in her

Asia DSheille

I found are all inside me

We have so much in common

We are really a lot alike

Isn't it just like the enemy?

To try and make us fuss and fight

But greater is he that is in me

Then he that is in the world

I'm going to do everything I can

To remain, Momma's precious girl!

Frances Roper '92

UNTITLED (2)

Wow! I love ya grandma which you never let me call-Naw I had to call you Nana.

I'm not mad though I never really learned about you 'til I was growing up and older.

After your sister Aunt Ann passed to be with you I guess, I learned some things that were the best.

Like your friends, gang, group "F-Troop",

Fighting. Nana I couldn't see that

Gangsta gallin', ready to slap.

Oh, but I am proud. It put things into perspective Like why at times I can be wreck less

But more important than that

I had to bring memory of you back.

And I'm tearing up as I write this

looking at my son you didn't know, so how could you miss?

I mean you left for heaven when I was only eight the very same year Taylor came

Now what's really rackin' my brain is that I'm fighting tears still feeling pain

Fourteen years later . . . . Grandma you're irreplaceable there is no one greater

What they don't know is before Jesus, you were my savior

When I was six, seven, eight you were teaching me prayers

Nana you know I can fill this page two pages with all I could say.

I didn't know this pain was still here or how much I still miss you,

But you still live through me-at least that's what people say

And as I feel pain it doesn't feel that way

I just love you Nana, I hope I told you enough

I love you

-Asia 2011

3 Generations...A grandmother-Minnie Dora Roper A mother-Frances Roper A daughter-Asia...1 Mind

For the grace of God
Thank you for Mothers

Thank you for a woman you so carefully prepared so large and generous using only one rib.

You filled her with such an enormous heart for the love she gives. Thank you Lord for letting her care, thank you for every child knowing even if no one else, she's always there.

Thankyou for molding such a chocolate dark beautiful piece of art, who has a huge brain to train us smart.

Thank you, for you have given me a head start. To have such a human with so many gifts in her heart. Is this why it takes nine months? While we're inside, are you training her Lord? Does she pass to get the best mother award?

For the grace of God, thank you for mom. You made her (from a 90s point) crucial, the bomb!

-Asia '98

3 Generations...A grandmother-Minnie Dora Roper A mother-Frances Roper A daughter-Asia...1 Mind

Letter To Sisters: Written 7/16/04

Dear sisters,

I am writing you all this letter to say,

I love you, you are beautiful, and hopefully we'll be in heaven one day.

Now don't get me wrong I do not have cancer or HIV,

but last look I opened my eyes and must share what I see.

Sisters we are dying left and right;

although you may think you are full of life.

Money has your love more than me so you sleep with men at night.

Oh I am dying too I've done it too I am by far not out of this fight.

But remember when you were my role model and I saw you with might.

Now I have grown up and things have changed:

You call me bitch, slut, hoe, and 2 x 4 my brain.

Now, you fight me at every chance

and roll your eyes at every glance.

It takes a village to raise one kid but you're still stuck on what I did; fornicate.

But remember when we kept it true,

and lifted up one another's blues.

Remember when we sang together in school said bump the teachers and broke the rules.

Now, I'm trying to teach. You say I am trying to preach and that I am a hypocrite,

but I remember when we prayed for each other and then we'd cry and sit.

Now all I do is talk and spit, but that's according to <u>you</u>.

For us to come to mutual hate is a point I never thought we would come <u>to</u>.

I do have mine and you do and have <u>yours</u>,

yet somehow I am the <u>whore.</u> I used to keep your kids, but now I'm off <u>shore.</u>

Now, I am in college and trying to work so can you help me <u>out</u>? Sister you say I am tit-for-tatting and I don't know what that's <u>about</u>.

Sister this isn't blood or relation in this letter to you all I <u>assure</u>, I just wish my sisters would come together in or out of Christ Love ya the 16th of July <u>2004</u>.

P.S.
Well work on the Christ part.

Past/Present

I like school, especially the subject of social studies.

It tells about history. Even though most school books are full of lies.

They tell how blacks did this and that and tell of the white man's needs and cries. But do they tell why the black man commits his crimes on white people—I don't think so they fail to disclose how they made our mothers maids and hoes.

They told many blacks they were old and not good. Since then gangs have formed and flipped hoods.

Crypts, bloods, vice-lords and what else blacks are going crazy, have lost their minds, do drugs, hoe and are killing themselves.

Who can I run to share this nation's pain? Obama hell no I wrote this originally in '95-you think much has changed?

Who can I run to if there is no one else? I run to self and reserve the right to preserve myself. Do I take the position middle finger everybody else? Sometimes it helps . . .

They killed Martin a true man. There's more resources/technology still less understand.

"guh" "young" "nigger" ignorant words from a to spam there is too much knowledge available now in our land, but we are weaker still how much longer?

I think what can I do I see the white man stronger . . .

Blacks, especially the young ones, hear other languages and think its crazy stupid dumb. I try but can't do it alone, try to educate these babies, but the parents don't help and it doesn't amaze me

'95(revised '11)

What I want to Be

As I sit home in my favorite chair, its school vacation and I don't know what happened to my hair.

I'm wondering what I want to be, I think a lot of things—

Especially a lawyer, not just a secretary.

That's not all, maybe someone who owns a mall.

I plan a future so I hope the US doesn't fall.

What do I want to be? I can already see me as a lawyer not just some secretary

There's another profession a marine biologist, I'd be very smart because it's hard to follow this.

Or maybe an actress in a play as a princess.

I want to get married and have a big wedding and my groom will carry me to my house that we will call heaven.

Then after the rest of my college years, I plan to save money so I can have kids. I plan a future what do I want to be? I can't see myself as just a secretary. I want a future so I can get a car, go to the moon, see the stars . . .

get united with my sisters again, with my family and friends from Maryland.

I am also African (far removed) and don't think the content of your character is the only thing applicants look through.

Even though slavery's over, there is still racism

and it's pretty dumb since it's only about the skin.

I want to be somebody I wonder what I'll be, maybe a lawyer not just a secretary!

-95

A dedication to the struggle of the black people

I respect all my fans, got to give em' a hand if they want to be down with my band, then let them stand.

They can put up a fight for their rights.

It's not right that during the night I see some white,

In blue, beating down a negro they never knew.

What gives them a right to mess with my peeps, they act like they own these streets.

Why they always on my peeps backs-well come in my boundary and you're not allowed, I'll take you off track plus you're bound to get slapped make you step back and don't expect no slack too many white folks like fighting with blacks.

So just go back to where you came from and

who should be the shamed one?

Not me, 'I don't care if you see me putting some minorities into the story to make it clear—too many whites have lied over the years.

Some want their children to think blacks are bad, but the way we get it done makes us look sad. (Yes we it's a humanity thing)

-95revised(2011)

Buddies

Most of your buddies are in school. You probably eat with them and play rope with them at recess. But do you really know who your buddies are? Do they make fun of you and say they were just playing "just saying"?

They're not your real buddies.

If they never laugh when other people make fun of you and they always ask your opinion for clothes and whether they are going to turn in an assignment or not, then they are probably your true buddy.

One way you can know if someone is not your buddy is if they get in trouble and say well it was him or her too,

that's not your buddy that's just a fool.

I have traveled three states in my eleven year old life and I've noticed from within, division with all US citizens. They will do anything to get to the top, lie to cops

Lying dimes dropped.

Even though some people care for their buddies such as me. I can not lie I don't appreciate when they steal, ask my friend please just keep it real

I tell my buddies just ask and I'll try to get it, or if I have it, I'll give it to them.

What about your buddies? Will they always be around or maybe they will let you down . . .

95

Teachers

Teachers!

In my whole life time from 4th—6th grade (my whole life I've had so far) teachers talk about how students fight and how they always have to hit back. Knowing they would probably do the same thing.

I'm not talking about just pushes, I can walk away from pushes, but girls be comin' up slapping you and boys making you trip up. What would you do teacher? Let them hit and harass you? I wouldn't, I didn't and I don't!

Work! Teachers like to give out lots of work, but all they do is look in the teacher's edition to check answers. It's so unfair how school work keeps you up late at night. You have to put forth a lot of effort, a lot of care to turn in assignments. Sometimes the teacher sends you away because he or she is busy and the assignment ends up being late, when the teacher is the person who made you wait!

That makes me mad and upset, but I still strive to do my best job yet.

I do what I must do to pass and talking and laughing isn't one of the task.

95

Why

Why should I feel so lonely most days? It didn't happen like that when I was in Maryland because I had my way.

Why should I feel the pain will never end? When I was in Maryland, I didn't feel like that because I had lots of friends.

Why should I feel bad? At my home in Maryland people comforted me when I was sad.

Why do I feel I can't trust anyone because in Maryland my days were full of fun?

Why should I have to be trapped in the house? Most days I go outside and some boys dissecting a squirrel or mouse.

Why do I have to wear certain colors outside?

because there are lots of gangs that spy.

Why are the black minds dead?

because the white man's words have been said.

Why!

95

Men

Some women say you can't live with or without men.

Most times I doubt men. I don't like when women let men abuse them and say it was my fault because I disapproved of him and his new job when they know that man is just a big slob. I've lived without a father for eleven years. Now it's too late for me to bother to shed any tears, especially on him, ha! This is what I think about some men.

Some men are ok, but it usually only last for one day. Some men do take care of their children, but act a fool towards their women. It's very hard to find a nice man and when you think you do, you see him holding some woman's hand. But wait, maybe it's his sister. Maybe her names Mary and you thought it was a sleazy secretary.

Some men can be scary. Like a man named Jim.

This is what I think about some men.

Don't worry, as long as your man gives you respect.

Train him like the little boy he acts like and you'll have him in check so, here is the end and that's what I think about some men.

95

BLACK MAN RUN BUT WHEN DO YOU STOP?

BLACK MAN, BLACK MAN DO YOU KNOW WHO YOU ARE?

BLACK MAN, BLACK MAN STOP TRYING TO RUN SO FAR.

PACE YOURSELF THAN PLACE YOURSELF AND DO NOT STOP UNTIL YOU THINK YOU ARE JUST GOING TO DROP.

YOU CAN'T RUN FOREVER, WHAT'LL YOU DO WHEN MOTHER NATURE CHANGES THE WEATHER?

BLACK MAN, BLACK MAN WHERE WILL YOU GO, WHAT WILL YOU BE?

YOU'LL NEED TO KNOW.

BLACK MAN BLACK MAN HOW CAN YOU RUN SO FAST?

BLACK MAN BLACK MAN, HOW LONG DO YOU THINK THIS ENERGY WILL LAST?

HOW CAN YOU STRIVE TO BE NUMBER 1 WHEN YOUR FLESH JUST TELLS YOU TO RUN, RUN, RUN?

WHAT ABOUT YOUR SPIRIT? WHAT RELIGION WILL YOU BE?

BAPTIST, BUDDHIST, OR MAYBE YOU'LL CHOOSE CHRISTIANITY!

BLACK MAN, BLACK MAN WHEN WILL YOU STOP TO HAVE A LIFE?

WHEN WILL YOU STOP TO HAVE A KID OR TWO AND A NICE WIFE?

BLACK MAN, BLACK MAN WON'T YOU SLOW DOWN TO A JOG, OR FLOW DOWN A STREAM ON A BIG OL' LOG?

BLACK MAN, BLACK MAN DO YOU KNOW WHERE YOUR HEADING?

WHEN WILL YOU REST YOUR HEAD ON A NICE PIECE OF BEDDING?

95

Games

Most people think when you talk about games, it's going outside or hide-and-go-seek. But the game I play is looking over life's peak. Whether or not I have the right to speak.

Most places you go have rules. Like no blacks, some places no whites and that's when you get into a major fight.

Life is like a game, played for fortune and fame. So many people do (play), would you?

When you go to an arcade, you have a plan already made and that is to win. Just like few defendants' trials end.

You have to sometimes play games just to get a decent job and pay and you think the game's over at the end of the day.

Wrong, you can't go and just change the song. Sometimes you keep the same song for a year because you can't quit your habits there's too much fear there.

Then you think it's over because you did your job or objective of the game, but you've earned so many points you go further up. If you're playing "Street Fighter" all you have to do is kick butt.

3 Generations...A grandmother-Minnie Dora Roper A mother-Frances Roper A daughter-Asia...1 Mind

But not in the game of life. That should be played day by day. And it's hard to get your way, especially when you don't want to play.

Then you get shot because of your fortune and fame and YES, now is the end of thegame.

'95

PEOPLE

I think about who the next black person will be to go every night and all I do is write. Although I want to be out there in the true fight.

I know some of these poems/thoughts talk about whites, but I'm 11 years old and what else am I suppose to think about when I see them bend our rights.

There's so much that I want to do, but in the South, I've noticed only whites rule.

I moved to Georgia from Maryland and to me the kids talk so funny. Some black kids (boys) in my class are either too lazy or too illiterate to divide two digit numbers into three digit numbers.

I'm wondering what has become of my people. They go out and kill and rob stores, when they only need to get a job.

3 Generations...A grandmother-Minnie Dora Roper A mother-Frances Roper A daughter-Asia...1 Mind

They are steady talkin' 'bout fight.

I write about how white people treat me and black people, but I won't call them out of their name because I don't like anyone calling me out of mine.

The way I see it is blacks and whites are so alike. I don't know why we have to fight.

I don't know why there are so many labels, so many different names, at the end of the day we all act like the same:

PEOPLE '95

Religion

Please get into a religion, it doesn't have to be mine. Get dedicated to something, you can do all the time.

Find yourself something you'll allow yourself to follow. Model the ways of your religion, so you can show others to be humble. And become lovers, so you can show 1 person love and the next, and 3 less people to worry about being vex.

Have confidence in our God or the supernatural power you believe in. and if all is well in your afterlife, you'll be rated a 10

Which is good, like 100%. Show everyone how that big rise in your life use to be dependent.

3 Generations...A grandmother-Minnie Dora Roper A mother-Frances Roper A daughter-Asia...1 Mind

Improve yourself, move others. Let it be nice for believers to look up to you, as you look up to him. His name is called religion.

-95

Gangs/feelings

G for the so called good gangs

A for all the good activities they've done

N for the negative community

G again for the

Super attempts-4-goodness

But . . . how can you spell gangs without a B for the bad gangs that kill, shoot, shank and think it's a thrill. Don't turn your back or cover your ears, listen, but what do you hear? Nothing because of silent tears.

Yes, over the years, I've got the knowledge

about the absence of mes in college.

Do you see what I see? Yes, that's the problem you see it, you hear it and try to deny, but yes fear it.

Parents discipline those children in gangs, incorrectly and say what more can I do?

I say make gang-control.

95

Peace

Peace, many people in this uncivilized nation cease to believe.

Mainly, the United States citizens treat it like it's a disease.

I've never gone one straight year without mourning heartache and bloodshed and tears.

Peace is of the least thought to go across your head. Do you not get tired of victims who end up dead?

Malpractice victims with herpes or AIDS in bed.

Whites and blacks going at each other's necks every day. Peace, peace is there any possible way?

That is what I ask myself …

Because when it comes to this racial situation everyone is at fault. Not just whites, not just blacks. We act like we are humans who've never been taught.

Everyone wants Politeness, Easy going, Access to a calm, Environment. PEACE

97

It's Not the Fault of a Child

Well what can the child do if mommy's threatening to ring her neck?

They say getting beat puts a child in check, but do you know the limit to not go pass?

If Kimmy makes a mess just whip her-Ask

me how I feel, because I do have an opinion about this

Nervous break downs, beat with fist,

Is it all called for when your child is only 2?

Yes I've seen it. Now what can I do?

Then they turn 3. Do you tell your kid brother "Stop following me!"

You damage him temporarily, so you don't have nothing to deal with

Abuse to so many parents is a myth

How about 4?

Children thrown into rooms with a never opening door.

And the worst things happen at 5,6, and 7

Raped, stabbed, bruised—used in the wrong ways!

No longer do they play

These are the cold days where they have to do chores

Learn how to clean, sometimes cook

Your parents in childhood are the # 1 crooks

No longer do you play, you grow smarter

What do I do? What can I say?

And in an odd and mysterious way,

A murder has been committed

And the child rest and lay.

97

Love and Insanity

So many people say the symptoms are the same,

the symptoms for insanity and love play.

Like insanity, love does not just go away

And like love, insanity is sometimes like a game.

Like when you have played me and I have gun aimed,

You have the nerve to reach out grab my neck and taste.

It turns you on when I cry and am mad in that place, thin line between love and hate I am ready to shoot your face.

Off course, no remorse, crazy in love with you.

You fool, dumb dude bringing me to do this to you.

I dislike you, it turns to hate crazily realizing you're not the man I thought you'd be,

Real love? No love. Marry you? INSANITY!

3 Generations...A grandmother-Minnie Dora Roper A mother-Frances Roper A daughter-Asia...1 Mind

Two Worlds

Yes, yes 2 world's is what I feel like I am stuck between

Doing good deeds in the dark or being evil and seen . . .

Yes, yes what many people do not know is that their friend in the light is in the dark a foe.

Monday through Saturday I am in a world of the world cursing, feeling good in my flesh, but sad in my spirit still I am compelled to sin.

On Sunday I go to church determined to change and be in the world you would have me to be in. Then backslide on Monday again. Again I am unable to win.

The battle is lost over and over, but I've been told the war is won! Don't worry.

In world number 2 my best friend says "Live your life girl-there's no hurry."

But my world one gets back burned to world two

And my weak flesh can not do it alone my spirit is calling you. Calling you . . .

7/09/04

A Pain So Deep

A pain so deep it hurts when you cry, a pain so deep it hurts when even your eyes are dry. It hurts so bad you even cry when you write, tears just fall out of nowhere on site. A pain more hurtful than no more breaths, worst than suffocation, annihilation, burning or bleeding to death too. Worst than getting shot. This is a pain deeper than the earth's core, deeper than the undiscovered ocean's floor, deeper than a black hole this is the pain of being alone. I ask God talk to me give me strength. Deliver me father I don't know how much more I can take. A pain so deep nobody loves me. My own mother, so called lover, is in love too deep but not towards me. We are wiser yet weaker just put me to sleep. I'm in pain I cry because you don't love me. Maybe I don't love you either. A pain so deep that no one knows, it's backed up cancer in my heart starting to show. It's killing me you see me cry and don't know why, you see me lash out and think I'm insane there is a war doctors call a conscience in my brain. It is not that, it is light and black. No!!! It's the devil he's trying to get me. And I'm crying feeling alone screaming please deliver me. I'm dying already inside and out, I'm so afraid what is that about? I used to fear nothing, I know it's him it's his unwanted presence it is Satin, leave me alone!! I won't kill myself. This pain is so far gone it has me crying for help. Sometimes I wish I just had enough courage to slit my wrists. My cries seem silent someone help me. I'm calling shouting hear me please. I'm spelling it too, G-O-D. Please don't forsake me. I'm yours God take me, the devil's trying to break me. Please I'm your baby. Raja, Jehovah, Ala save me.

I've been raped of life, purity, I'm crazy a knife is sharp, Oh Lord save me.

Gabriel, Michael, Perez saved me.

2001/2002 (revised 2011)

Life and Death

I forgot that quickly,

Washing dishes I was inspired by my seed.

Here's a message for you, Perez, from me:

Perez live your life take your time, not quickly.

Never ever worry about me,

Mommy lives her life live yours freely.

Please don't worry, be more healthy than me,

Do your thing child, get started promptly.

'No bother worry'-mommy does me and when I die that's part of life you see.

I love you Perez don't forget me,

But death comes after life don't worry about mommy . . .

(or life after death, heaven)

Girl

Why am I doing it really? Perhaps because it's the way. I try to right my wrongs, but can't think straight.

No write my wrongs, I'll often be incorrect and am far from perfect, I haven't arrived yet.

So many . . . too many I've even forgot names. The pictorial memory picture is gone with no frame.

Stop approaching me–but Asia you're beautiful. Beautiful enough for what? I still am not full.

Call me half empty not full, incomplete–well maybe you need to be alone, over a hundred contacts in the phone and none of them grown? Still the house is no home.

I admit it I do not love you, I like you a little, but you're just a fool. Sometimes I just don't want to be approached or walked up to. It has everything to do with me and nothing to do with you.

I am broken, perhaps there's no cure, surely no prince charming, of this I'm so sure.

2008

Because They Raped Our Babies . . .

Was about two years ago (2009) I realized this-

Something that troubled me, bothered me, made me pissed

See I live in DC the peculiar thing is-

how many of my neighbors have been raped and are now rapist

But a couple of years ago a class trip-

to the Blacks and Wax in B-more told some of what went down on ship

Portuguese, French, Europeans of some sort

Disgusting taboo demonic F-u-c-k-ed who they did port

Over some 400 years ago and even before the Mid-Atlantic Trade our babies were degraded, sodomized and RAPED

And if you think it's not here in a prevalent state

Take a look at congress today 5/6 states "should we marry those who are gay?"

An unspoken, unasked question back in the day

Because they raped our babies is what I say

Yes I know same sex partners today

Yes most of them came from a background of prey

Yes most will say their lifestyle is okay

And that's what Crow laws said about slavery 'cuz it did pay

I say leave it to God to make the call on that play

3 Generations...A grandmother-Minnie Dora Roper A mother-Frances Roper A daughter-Asia...1 Mind

And would I want it for my babies NO WAY

That is my choice, as for me and my house is what I'll say—2011

So Remember to Call her Beautiful

There are so many pretty girls in DC says Wale. Yes pretty girls, but is that where they stay?

I too was once a pretty girl, roughed around coal inside diamond, clamshell pearl.

Do you know the pressures you put on her? Because she won't sex, you dumped her. Her vagina is not what makes her beautiful.

It's her intelligence she tries to share- look what she does to you.

It is not that she is a crack-head now; it's that after he beat her she got up after she fell down.

Remember to call her by her name and understand her mind, no games.

It is that after the fact, of her aborting a baby her God-fearing mamma told her to, she bounced back. Yes, she has to live with that.

She is coming of age with no father in sight, she fights, makes honor roll, does so many things right.

It's not that she wanted to be a teen-age mother; she was simply searching for love, so simply just love her.

And remember to call her beautiful often, she'll be called bitch, slut, hoe, nigger, trick many times before she reaches her coffin.

Remember to call her beautiful, by her name not just Boo. Is that all your mother is? A piece of pie to you?

Respect your mother. Beautiful is a reflection of your mother too. She could have decided to just kill you.

Our young ladies having babies, tricking for money, "Hustler save me."

Maybe, just maybe if you called her Beautiful she wouldn't act crazy.

She is certainly beautiful if after you raped she . . .

Daddy, uncle, why penetrate me? I am beautiful, your niece your baby.

Sodomized, a thousand lies, so many cries, broke family ties, shit smelling hide, parents too high, society too jive . . . she's been through so much in her short life . . . please remind her all the time, all the time that she is fine, not appearance, but has a fine mind and that when the world falls back and reclines . . . her energy, poise, levels are so full-so remember often to call her beautiful.

Who is Jesus?

Who is Jesus so many want to know the man the spirit the ultimate show

What is Jesus so many people ask although athtiest non-believers would not pay the tax

Who is Jesus? I once heard Jesus was a "he" a "man" a lion,

The creator and connecting key to the Lord ZION.

What is Jesus? I heard Jesus was the thing, a spirit so powerful and plenty forgiving with the spirit it brings.

Who is Jesus? I heard he was me, I heard he was you when we are lovingly.

Better yet, when we love in our will because it's his will

True love always seals the deal . . .

What is Jesus? Someone who's a thing who is OH! so real

The pump in the heart of the mother of Emmitt

Till

The rag sponging up blood the dark city spills

The light in the non-bright of black hole chill

Calm enough to be quiet before the storm but zealous enough to be zeal.

Who is Jesus? One said he is the savior the Christ the breath after death the doctors said there was no more life.

Jesus, Joshua, Joseph, Moses

Enough for the nay sayers who cry his name near death but in wealth have their non-chalant supposes

Situated too too comfortably to know or not know the excellent, exalted being who is he

Undeniably, unequivocally not a UFO

Sadly enough there's so many who don't know, don't know if they know, don't know if they know, don't know if they know . . .